It's GOOD to be a BOY!

JOSEPH SPURGEON

To Charles, Calvin, Rocky and Ezra

Published by 5 Solas Press | 5solaspress.com

ISBN: 978-1-7349194-0-0

Special thanks to Mara-Lee Lapp Strickler. Her creativity helped form the vision for this project and inspired the final artwork throughout.

An Appeal to Fathers

Fatherhood is an incredible gift from God. The Bible teaches us that God the Father bestows His name of "father" on imperfect men like you and me. This authoritative blessing comes with tremendous responsibility to represent God to your family. Your sons need you especially in a time when masculinity is under attack.

Whether it is the constant warnings against "Toxic Masculinity" or the cries to "Smash the Patriarchy", our culture is in rebellion to God's design for men and women. If masculinity cannot be indoctrinated away, we treat it as a disease to be medicated against. According to the National Institute of Mental Health, boys are three times more likely to be diagnosed with ADHD.[1] Mark Hancock rightly diagnosed the problem:

> Conduct that used to be considered typical boy behavior—running or climbing when it's not appropriate, or having a hard time waiting to talk or react—is now bulleted in lists of ADHD symptoms, as if boyhood is some sort of social disease that needs to be eradicated. In a culture wary of "toxic masculinity" and bombarded with decades of secular media presenting fathers and husbands as buffoons, is it any wonder that psychologically damaging, unscientific gender-identification propositions find an audience? Boys are starved of moral direction and ignored in terms of academic struggles. They have no platform for their own defense because they've already been judged deficient.[2]

This has left a whole generation of young men caught in a perpetual adolescence, their highest calling to play video games and hang out with the bros. Young men are not pursuing marriage, fatherhood, or vocation. They do not know what it is to be a man.

The Bible teaches us that it is good to be a man. When God created man and put him in the garden, He called it very good (Genesis 1:37). He even named the species after the male. "God created man in His own image, in the image of God He created him; male and female He created them" (Genesis 1: 27). Masculinity is good and you have a great responsibility to teach your sons that it is good.

It is my hope that this book will be a tool to help you teach your sons God's purpose and what it means to be a man.[3] What is that purpose? It is to glorify God by being a builder, provider, protector, fighter, leader, worshipper, and proclaimer. Because God has hardwired these purposes into your son's nature, he can only either distort them and use them for selfish purposes in rebellion to God, or use them for his glory by faith in Christ Jesus.

Your son will either work to build up the kingdom of God or he will work to build up his own worthless kingdom. He will either provide for his family or provide for his own lusts. He will either protect the vulnerable or protect his self-interests. He will either fight the devil, his sinful flesh, and worldly systems or he will fight *for* the devil, his sinful flesh, and worldly systems. He will either lead others to God in obedience or he will lead in rebellion to God, which many men do by a passive willingness to be led by women. He will either worship the one true and triune God or he will worship idols and false gods. He will either proclaim the truths of God or he will proclaim the lies of this world.

As you read this book to your son, take the time to talk about each God-given purpose. To help with your discussion, I am providing scripture references below for each truth. In addition to reading this book, it is important to model the truth. Your son needs to see you living out your God-given masculinity. In a time when the very idea of manhood is considered toxic, your son needs to see that it is good to be a boy. May God give you and your son strength to stand firm in the faith and act like men (1 Corinthians 16:13).

—Joseph Spurgeon, *June 2020*

NOTES:

1 "Attention-Deficit/Hyperactivity Disorder (ADHD)." National Institute of Mental Health, November 2017. https://www.nimh.nih.gov/health/statistics/attention-deficit-hyperactivity- disorder-adhd.shtml.

2 Hancock, Mark T. Let Boys Be Boys. Youth Adventure Program, INC., 2018.

3 Some readers may be put off by references to firearms and abortion ministry in this book. But these are not carelessly placed in a children's book but rather intentionally designed so as to provide fathers with opportunities to talk about gun safety, self-defense, and the plight of the preborn.

7 Reasons God Made Men

Build

Genesis 2:15, Genesis 3:17-19, 2 Thessalonians 3:10, Colossians 3:23, 1 Thessalonians 4:11-12, Proverbs 10:4, 2 Thessalonians 3:7-9, 2 Thessalonians 3:12, John 5:17, Proverbs 24:30-34, 1 Chronicles 22:15, Proverbs 14:23, Ecclesiastes 9:10, Proverbs 12:24, Proverbs 12:11, Proverbs 22:29, Matthew 6:33, Psalm 90:17, Psalm 127, Ecclesiastes 3:22, Exodus 35:10

Provide

1 Timothy 5:8, 2 Thessalonians 3:10, Deuteronomy 24:5, Ephesians 5:25, Ephesians 5:28-30, 1Timothy 3:1-5, Proverbs 18:9, Ephesians 4:28, Proverbs 13:22, 1 Corinthians 15:58, Acts 20:35, Psalm 128, Proverbs 21:20, Leviticus 23:22

Protect

John 15:13, Exodus 22:2-3, Nehemiah 4:14, Genesis 14:14-16, Exodus 2:17-19, Numbers 30:3-16, Psalm 18:2, Luke 22:35-38, Esther 8:10-12, Nehemiah 4:16-23, Psalm 68:5, Psalm 41:1-3, James 1:22-27, Proverbs 24:10-12, Job 29:7-17

Fight

1 Timothy 6:12, Deuteronomy 3:22, Nehemiah 4:14, Joshua 10:25, 1 Samuel 4:9, Jeremiah 1:19, Zechariah 10:5, 1 Timothy 1:18, 2 Timothy 4:7, Philippians 2:25, 2 Timothy 2:3-4, Philemon 1:2, 2 Corinthians 6:1-10, 2 Corinthians 10:3-5, Ephesians 6:10-18, 2 Samuel 22:31-41, Psalm 18, Psalm 144:1-2, Joshua 1:9

Lead

Genesis 1:26-28, Genesis 18:19, Numbers 30, Deuteronomy 5:16, Deuteronomy 6:5-7, Deuteronomy 27:1, Deuteronomy 32:46, Proverbs 2:1. Proverbs 3:1, Proverbs 6:20, Ephesians 6:1-4, Exodus 12:26-27, Proverbs 19:18, Proverbs 22:6, Ephesians 5:25-32, 1 Timothy 3:1-16, 1 Timothy 2:12, 1 Peter 3:1-6, Colossians 3:18, 1 Corinthians 11:3, 1 Timothy 3:12, 1 Corinthians 14:34, Exodus 18:21, 1 Timothy 4:12, Hebrews 13:17, Hebrews 13:7, Ephesians 5:22

Worship

2 Chronicles 20:21, Colossians 3:16, Ephesians 5:19, Psalm 147:1, John 4:23-24, Romans 12:1-2, Psalm 95:6, Revelation 4:11, Romans 12:1, Luke 4:8, Matthew 4:10, Psalm 99:5, Exodus 20:3, Acts 16:25, Matthew 2:11, Daniel 4:37, Psalm 100:4, Psalm 100:2, Psalm 95:1-6, Psalm 66:4, 1 Chronicles 16:29, Revelation 19:10, James 5:13

Proclaim

Matthew 28:18-20, Psalms 71:17-18, Psalms 78:4-7, Mark 16:15-16, Luke 24:47-48, Acts 1:8, James 1:27, 2 Corinthians 5:18-19 , Matthew 5:16, Proverbs 11:30, Matthew 10:32, Luke 14:23, James 5:20, Ezekiel 33:1-9, Matthew 5:13-16, Ephesians 5:11, Proverbs 8:13, Psalm 97:10, Romans 12:9, 1 John 3:16-17, Psalms 82:4

"The father of the righteous shall
greatly rejoice: and he that begetteth
a wise child shall have joy of him."

Proverbs 23:24

Hello, I'm Charles. That's my dad!
I am a boy. It is good to be a boy.

Why is it good to be a boy?
Well, let me tell you….

It's good to be a boy because
God made boys to be builders.

I get to work real hard with my dad
to build my tree house.

My dad goes to work every day.
He works so that we have food,
clothes, and a house.

It's good to be a boy because
God made boys to be providers.

It's good to be a boy because
God made boys to be protectors.

My dad says that when I get older he will teach me how to use his gun so I can protect my family. But for now, I protect my club house with my cap gun. It always scares away the big bad wolf.

It's good to be a boy because
God made boys to be fighters.

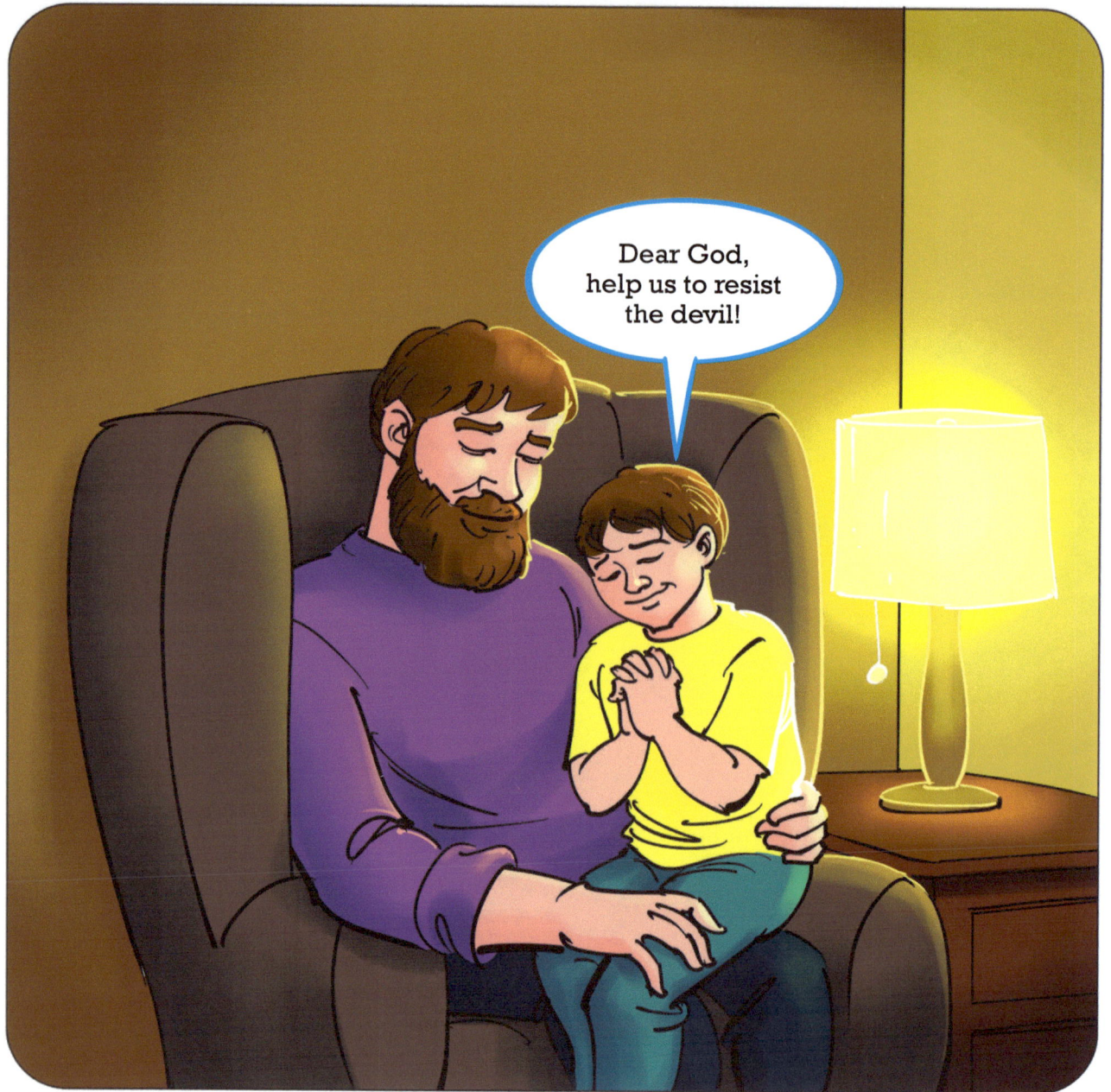

We have an enemy to fight—the devil!
We don't use guns and fists. We fight him
with prayer and the Word of God.

My dad is the leader in our home. He leads us because he loves us and God wants us to obey him. One day, I will lead just like him.

11

It's good to be a boy because
God made boys to be leaders.

It's good to be a boy because
God made boys to be worshipers.

And it is good to worship Him.

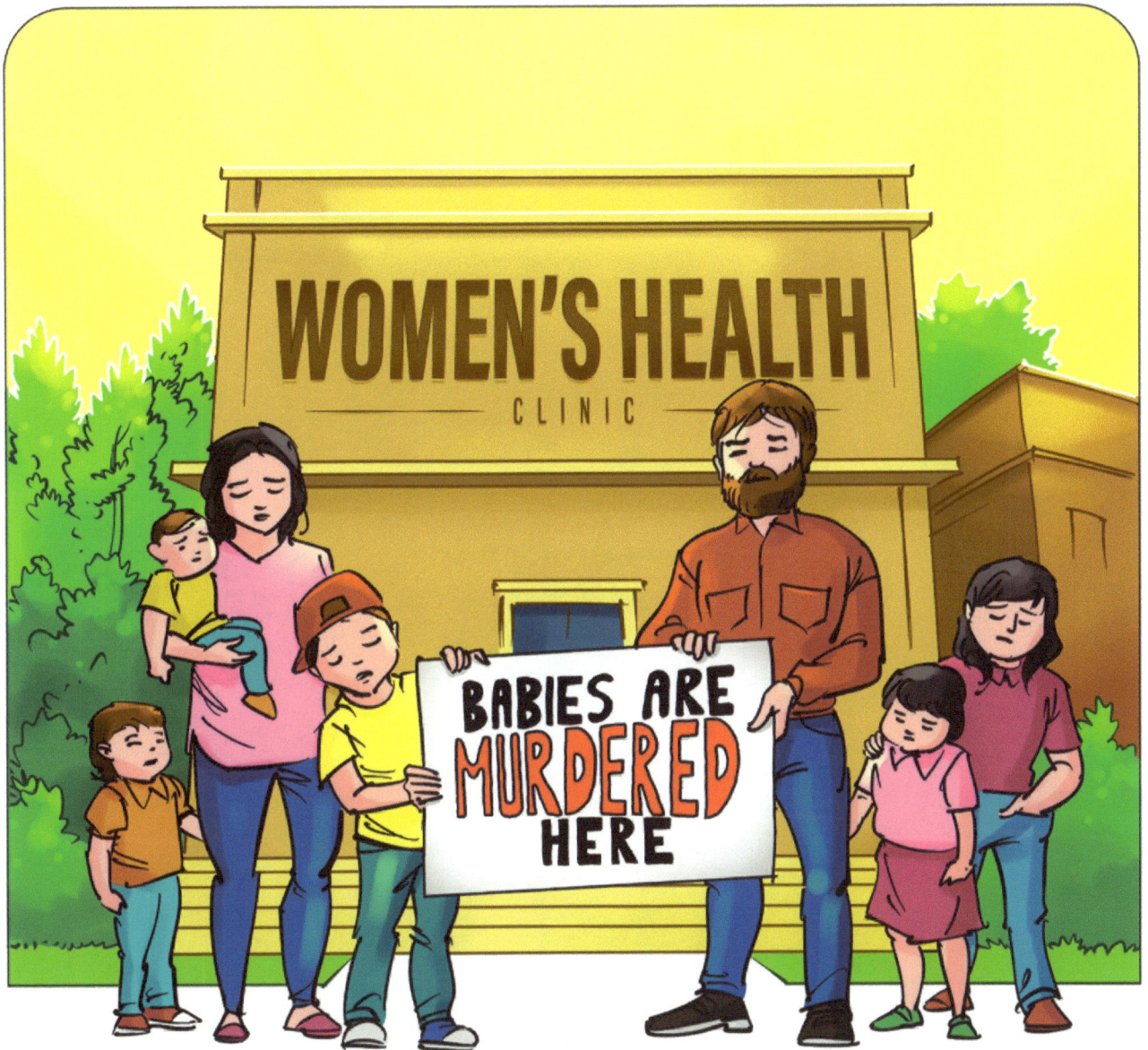

Because God has been so good to us,
we should proclaim the truth wherever we can.
I love to tell people about Jesus.

15

It's good to be a boy because God
made boys to be proclaimers.

I am thankful that God made me because…

17

It's GOOD to be a BOY!

18

www.ingramcontent.com/pod-product-compliance
Lightning Source LLC
Chambersburg PA
CBHW042015090426
42811CB00015B/1653